Daryl Cagle's "Donald Trump and the Republicans" Coloring Book!
Artwork and text by Daryl Cagle

Published by Cagle Cartoons, Inc.
ISBN-13: 978-0692702147
ISBN-10: 0692702148
Printed in the United States of America, First Printing: May, 2016

Donald Trump Plants the Flag

Having scaled the Republican mountain, the Donald plants the flag of victory.

DARYL
CAGLE
.com

Donald Trump's Immigration Plan

Trump says his plan to deport all "illegal aliens" is similar to a plan from the 1950's called "Operation Wetback." Looney Tunes characters are from the 1950's, too.

Donald Trump and the Media Circus

The media clowns chase after Trump's every word.

DARYL CAGLE

POLITICALCARTOONS.COM

Donald Trump Rockets to the Nomination

It isn't only Democrats who "feel the burn."

DARYLCAGLE.COM   POLITICALCARTOONS.COM

Donald Trump and Abortion

Trump wants to change the Republican platform regarding abortion to include exceptions for rape, incest and the health of the mother, angering "pro-lifers."

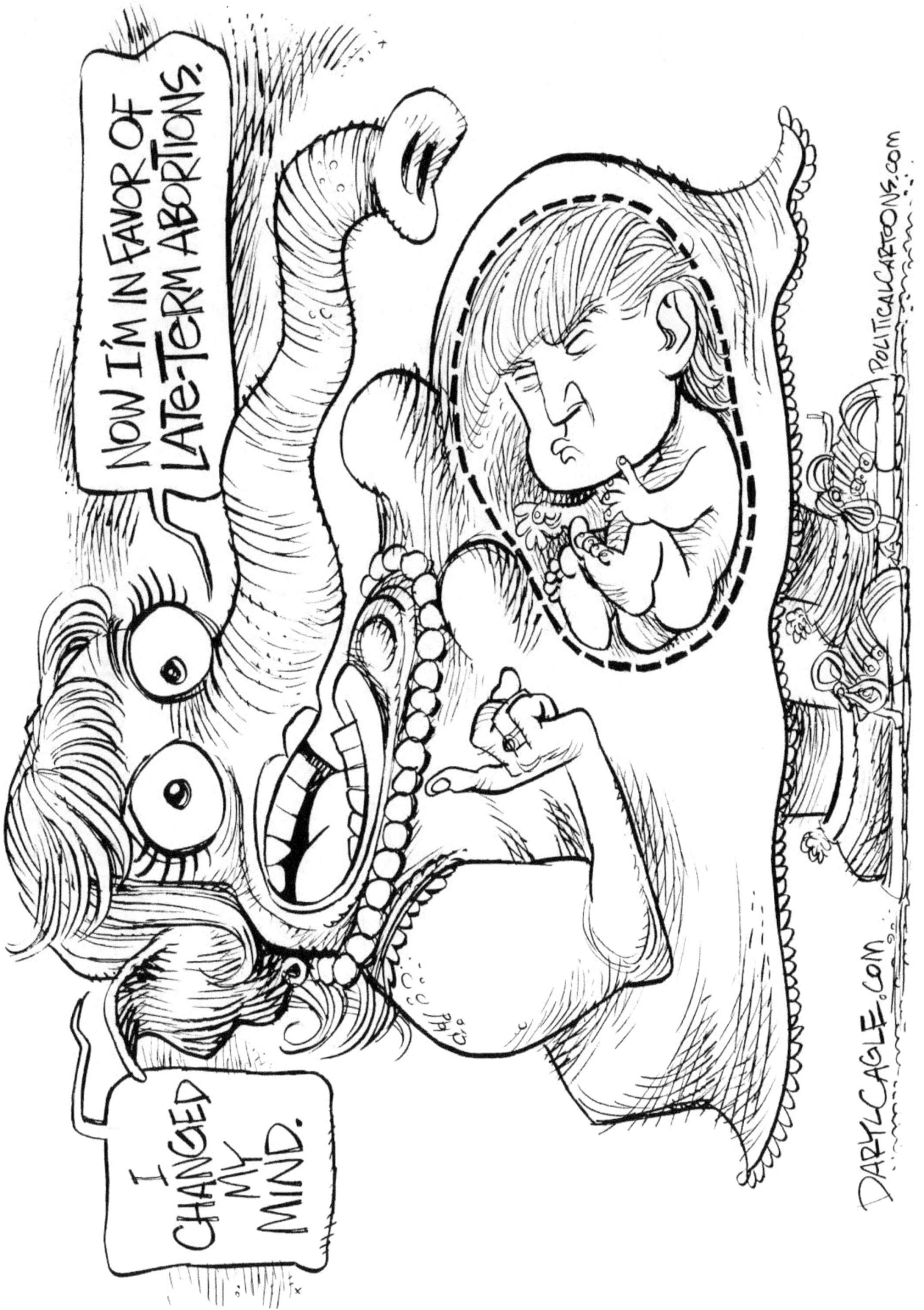

NOW I'M IN FAVOR OF LATE-TERM ABORTIONS.

I CHANGED MY MIND.

DARYLCAGLE.COM

POLITICALCARTOONS.com

Donald Trump and the "Party of Lincoln"

Republicans like to think of themselves as the "Party of Lincoln," but Lincoln himself might not like thinking of himself as a Republican these days.

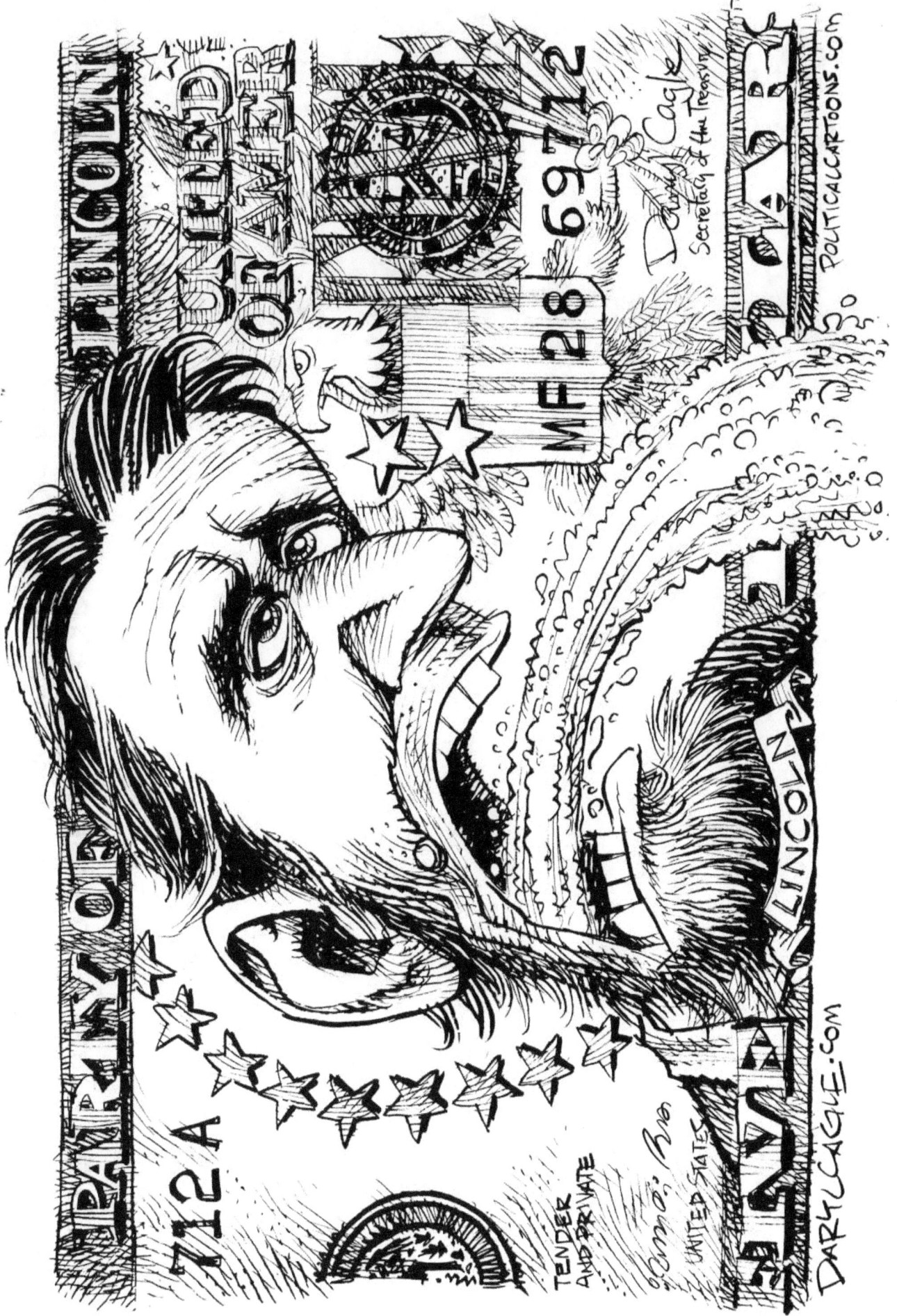

Donald Trump's Foreign Policy Experts

The Donald says he consults with himself about foreign policy matters.

STOP FOOLING AROUND AND JUST TAKE ISIS OUT—AND KEEP THOSE MUSLIMS OUT UNTIL WE CAN FIGURE OUT WHAT'S GOING ON!

INVISIBLE FOREIGN POLICY ADVISOR.

DARYLCAGLE .COM

POLITICALCARTOONS.COM

Donald Trump Ties the GOP Up in Knots

The Republican party struggles with disagreements about Trump.

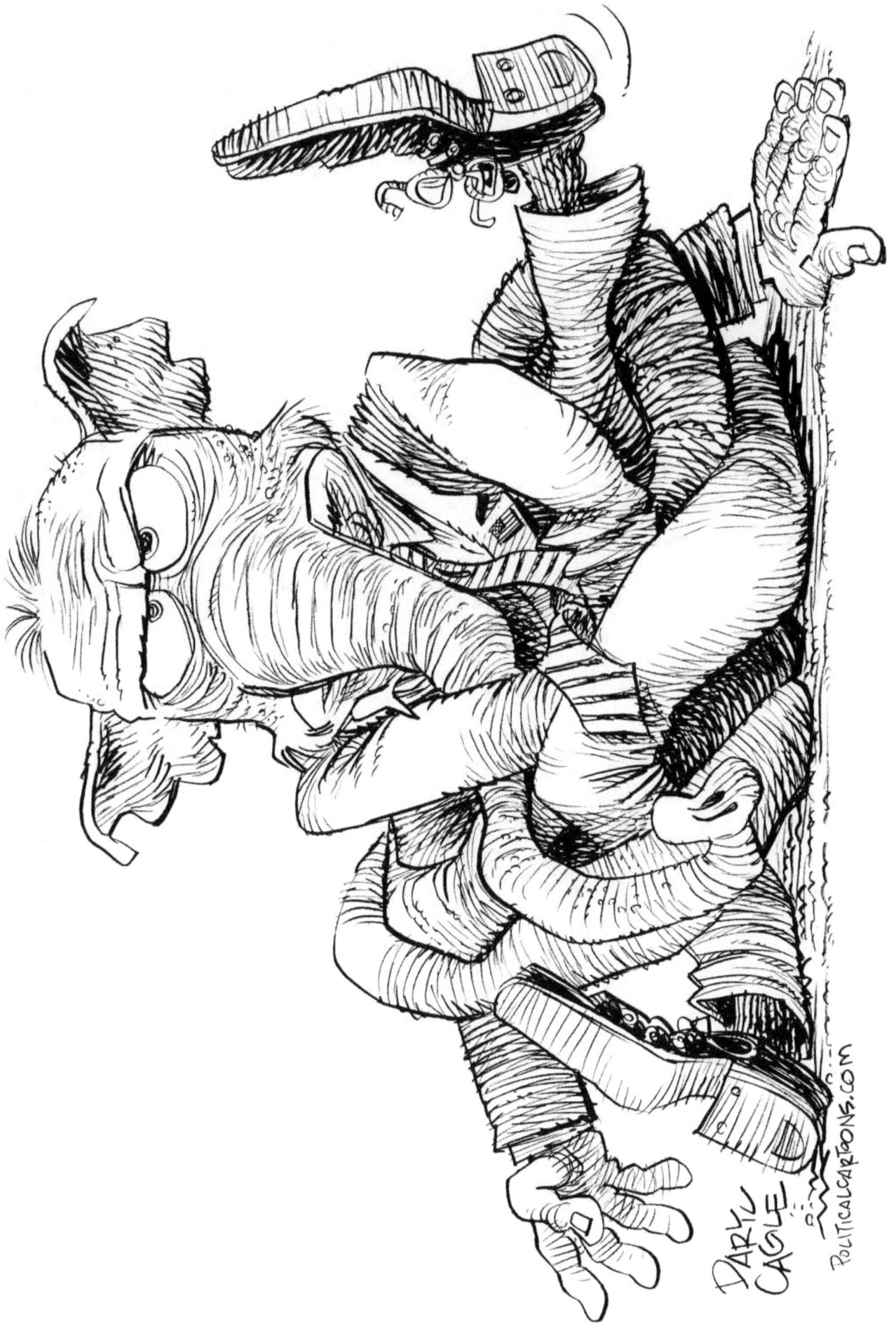

Donald Trump and the GOP Smoke Filled Room

The Donald accuses the Republican establishment bosses of making rules that favor their preferred, non-Trump candidates.

Donald Trump Really Said THAT?

The eager, anti-Trump media loves to declare that the Donald has sunk his campaign when he says something new that offends someone.

Donald Trump Turns Republicans Against Each Other

It looks like the Republican party may be doomed.

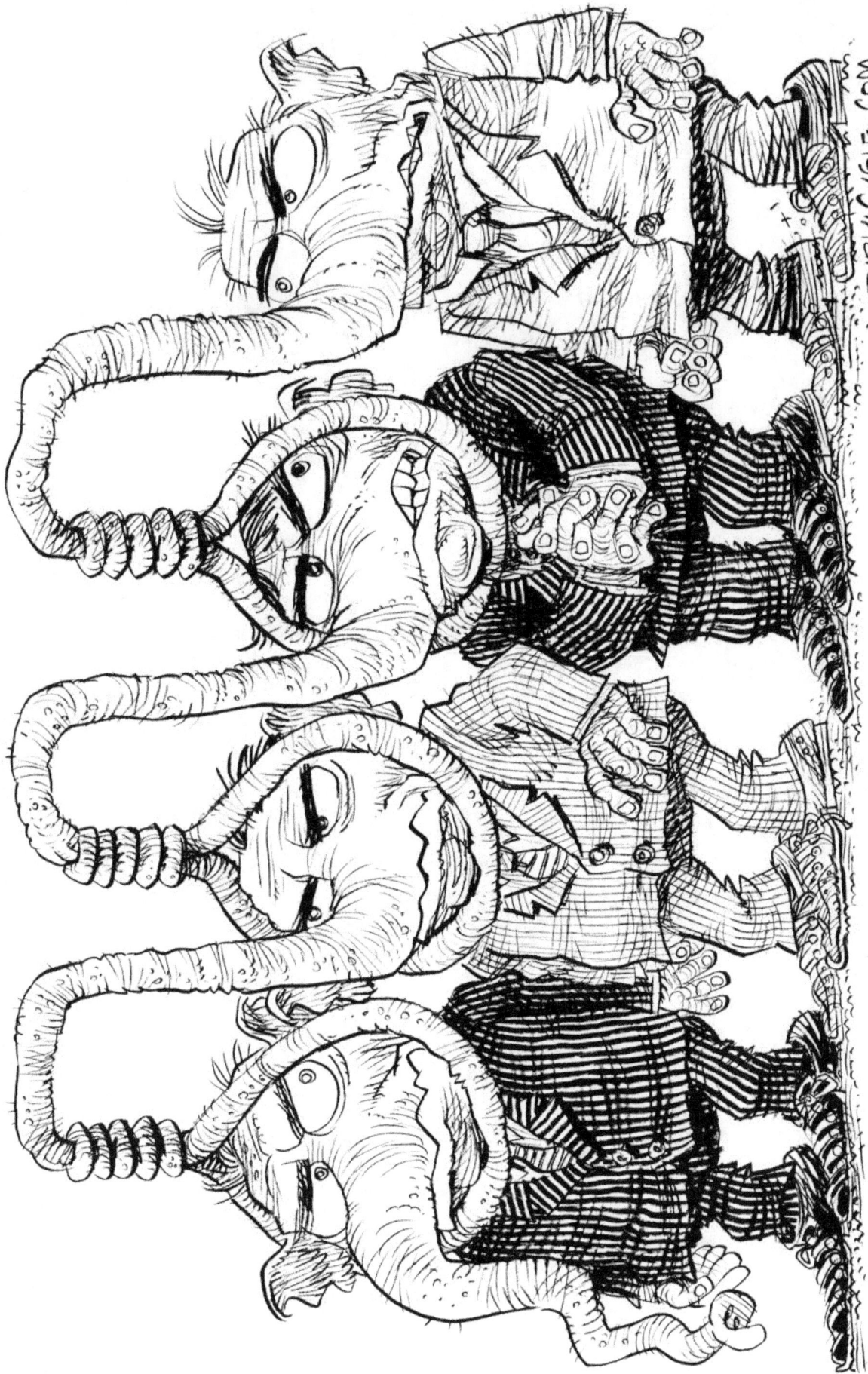

Donald Trump Races

Trump complains about establishment Republicans making up rules to stop him from winning the race to the White House.

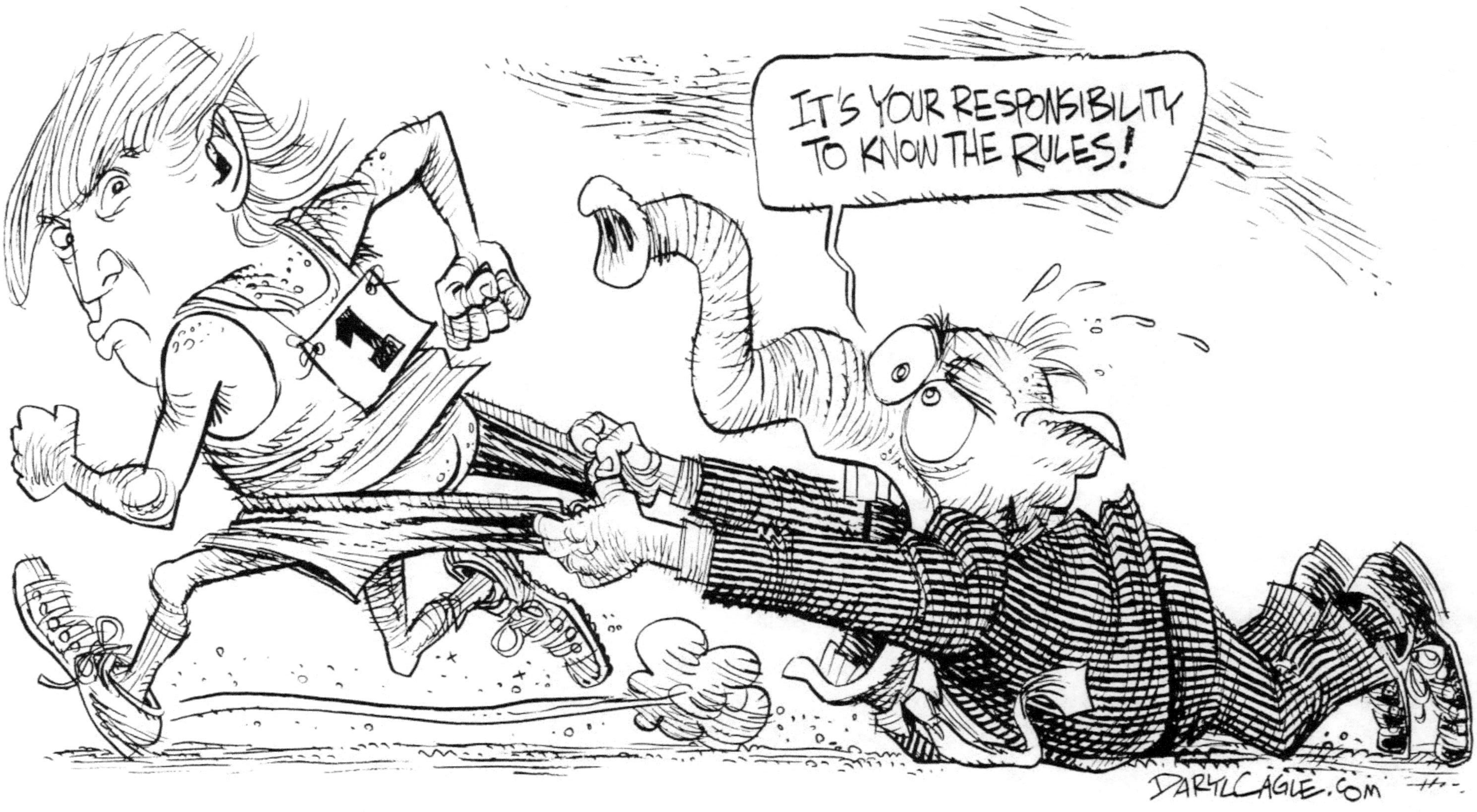
IT'S YOUR RESPONSIBILITY TO KNOW THE RULES!
DARYLCAGLE.COM

Donald Trump and and the Media

Whatever the media says to sink Trump, voters don't care.

Donald Trump Skipped a Debate with Megyn Kelly

As part of a feud with Fox News Anchor, Megyn Kelly, Trump skipped one of the debates.

TRUMP

DARKCAGLE.com

POLITICALCARTOONS.com

Donald Trump the Pied Piper

The cartoon was supposed to recall the Pied Piper leading the children out of town. Readers thought it was about leading "the rats out of town."

Donald Trump and Jeb Bush

Trump dispatched his chief rival, Jeb Bush, early in the campaign by tying him to the failures of his brother, President George W. Bush.

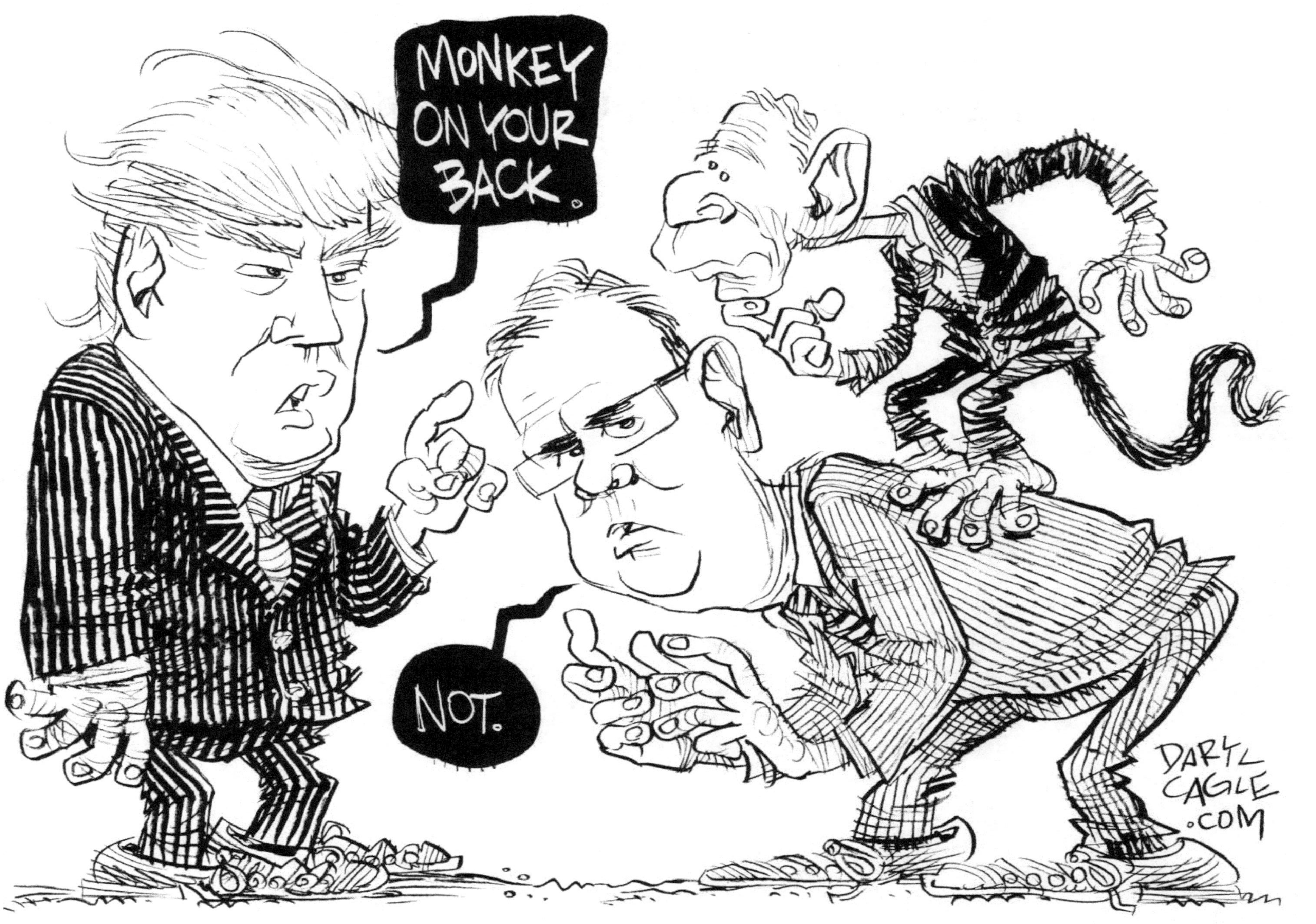
MONKEY ON YOUR BACK.
NOT.
DARYL CAGLE .COM

Donald Trump Supporters Don't Do as They Are Told

Republican big-shots are frustrated that they can't sway voters away from Trump.

Donald Trump May Break Up the GOP

The cracks are showing in the Republican party.

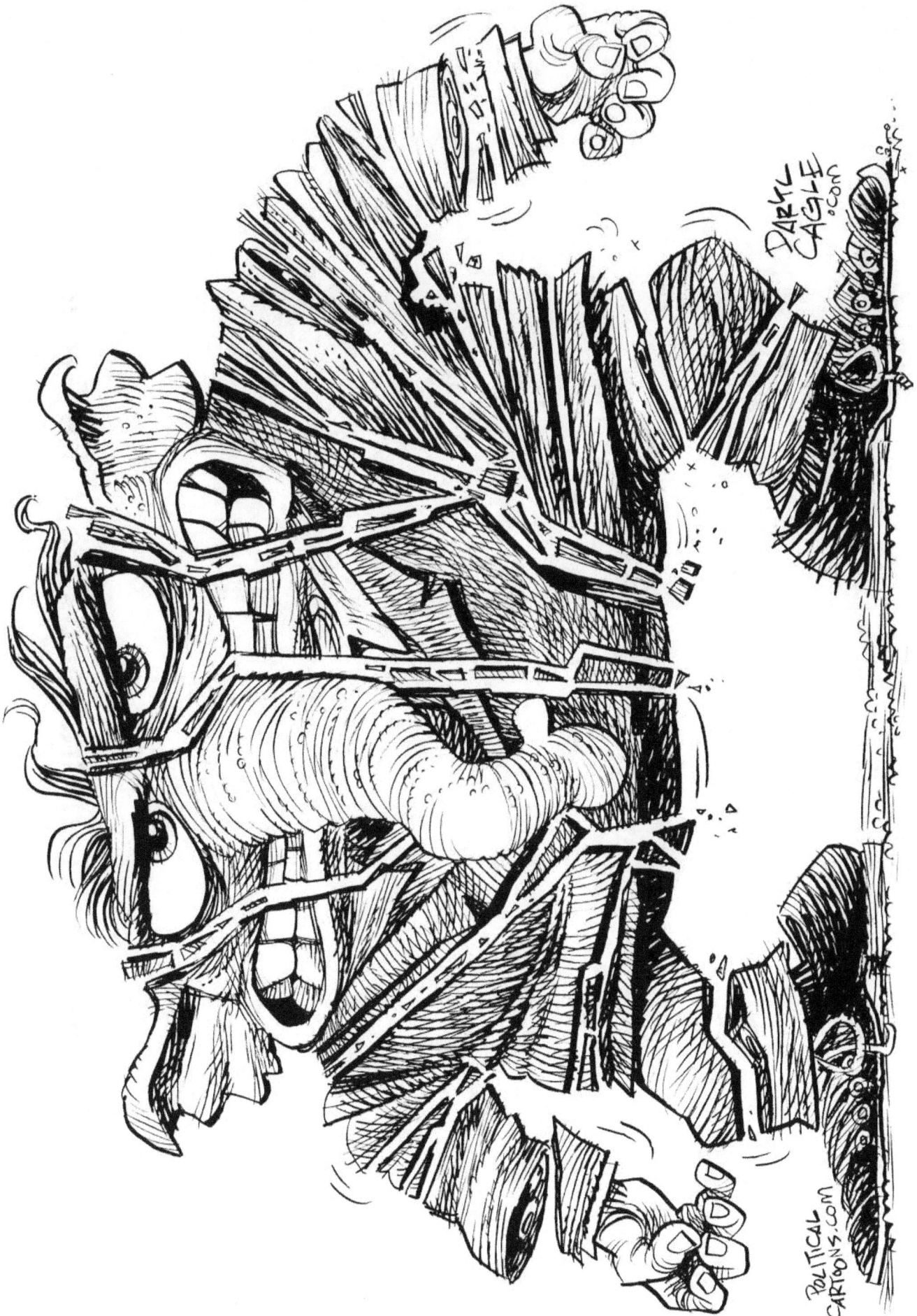

Donald Trump, Lyin' Ted Cruz and Oscar the Grouch

All are grouchy.

APOLOGIES TO SESAME STREET

I'LL VOTE FOR WHOEVER IS GROUCHIER.

DARYL CAGLE.COM

Donald Trump, Republicans and Refugees

The Donald wants to keep Syrian refugees out of the USA. The other Republicans all seem to agree with him on this.

THANKS TO MICHAEL KOUNTOURIS

Trump Dispatches his GOP Critics

Many irritating Republicans were reluctant to support Trump, but The Donald dealt with them, scratching those annoying itches.

Donald Trump and Republican Harakiri

Trump's success may skewer the GOP.

DARYLCAGLE.com
POLITICALCARTOONS.com

Donald Trump the Strongman

With a string of primary victories, the Donald seems unstoppable.

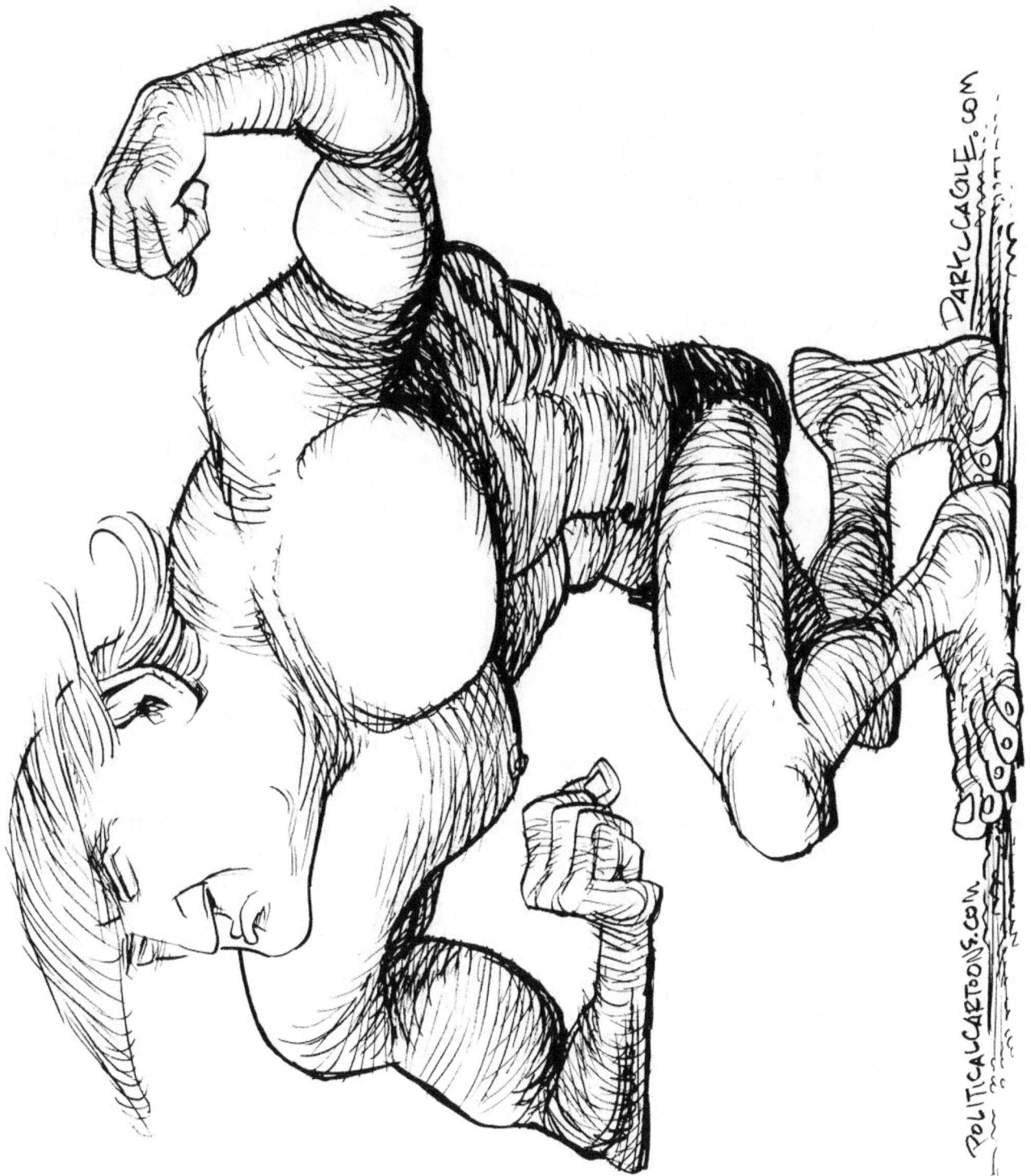

For the past 35 years, Daryl Cagle has been one of America's most prolific cartoonists. He worked for 15 years with Jim Henson's Muppets, illustrating scores of books, magazines, calendars, and all manner of products. Daryl still sees pigs, frogs, Sesame Street and Fraggle Rock characters when he closes his eyes. He worked as the editorial cartoonist in Hawaii, then was the cartoonist for the Washington Post's Slate.com site and msnbc.com. Daryl is America's most widely syndicated editorial cartoonist.

To see more of Daryl's work visit DarylCagle.com. To reprint cartoons from Daryl and from the top editorial cartoonists around the world, visit PoliticalCartoons.com or call (805) 969-2829.

Collect All of the Daryl Cagle Coloring Books at CagleBook.com

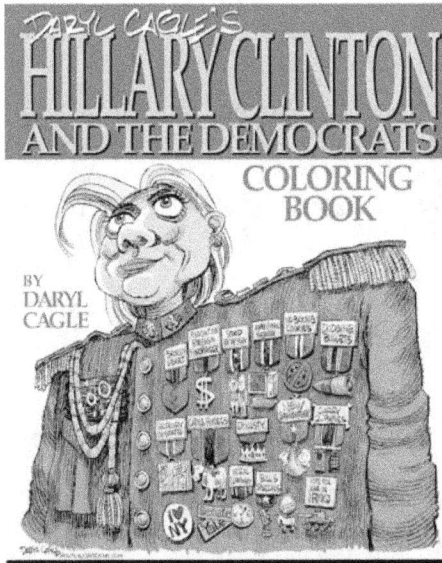

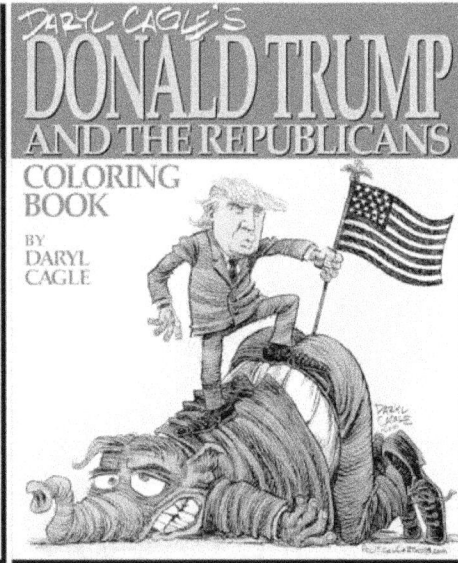

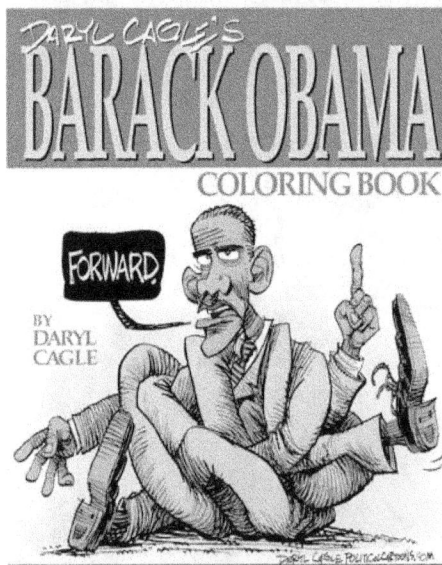

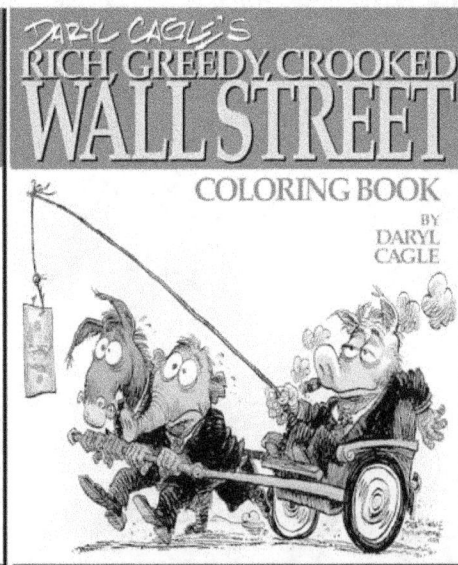

* 9 7 8 0 6 9 2 7 0 2 1 4 7 *